Abby Alligator is ready to work.
What will Abby do?

Abby wants to be an acrobat.

But she's afraid of falling.

Abby wants to be an artist.
But she can only paint apples.

Abby wants to be an animal doctor.
But she's allergic to aardvarks.

Abby wants to be an astronaut.

But she meets an angry alien.

Abby wants to be an actor.

But she is awful.

Abby can't think of any other jobs.

Then Abby has an AMAZING idea.
"I'll be an author!" Abby says.

Abby Alligator writes all about her adventures
as an acrobat, an artist, an animal doctor,
an astronaut, and an actor.

Being an author is AWESOME!

How many things can you find that begin with the letter A?

14

Aa Cheer

A is for alligator and acorns on trees

A is for "Ah-choo!" when you sneeze

A is for apples baked in a pie

A is for airplane up in the sky

Hooray for A, big and small—

the most awesome, amazing letter of all!